THE CREATIVE COMPANY
Third Edition

ANDERS HEMRE

CONTENTS

FORWARD TO THE THIRD EDITION

It's been a few years since this book was first published. Today, innovation is as urgent as ever. Looking at the world around us, one would not have expected anything else. At the same time, many challenges seem to remain the same as organizations try to compete and pursue growth through innovation. So, even if a few references date back a while, the general conclusions and suggestions of this book's original text still apply.

Creativity is a human characteristic closely related to curiosity and ingenuity. It never rests. And in "a world awash with ideas" as professor Roberto Verganti at the Polytechnic University of Milan likes to put it, *direction* becomes crucial to innovation. Direction channels creativity into useful innovations. More or better of the same don't create new markets or consumer "wows". But in our pursuit of direction we need to not only look for the right ideas but also for the right people. And for the right people to thrive, they need to be in the right environment. Individuals open to change e.g. may perform better in opportunity spotting, while the more conservative do better in activities such as idea screening and stage gate reviews. Innovation work can be organized in different ways. Business environments change. Leaders come and go. But creativity, control and expertise always have to coexist and combine as innovation moves new ideas from mind to market.

Successful companies don't just innovate, but innovate better. They innovate for certain reasons and with certain objectives in mind. Strategies may be more or less well articulated and successful innovations may occur even without a strategy. On the other hand, ignoring - or going wrong with - strategy could certainly be fatal also to an otherwise innovative business. Companies wanting to improve their business by improving their innovation performance need to pay attention.

When Sony Mobile Communications in recent years tried to make a broader and more systematic effort to innovate and create new business, they realized that this required not only the strengthening of innovation management practices but also a change in structure, policies and mindset. Even openness and spontaneity need certain boundaries, such as orderly processes, plans and rules to flourish. That's why creative companies don't just have more ideas. They also accomplish more with the ideas they have. They become more competitive and they improve their business performance. And they collaborate well.

Knowledge creators and businesses need each other. Therefore, co-creation and co-innovation in ecosystems play increasingly important roles and Open Innovation has become a widely adopted practice and in some industries even a structural change.

Other developments also profoundly impact innovation and innovation management.

Artificial Intelligence is a deeply transformative technology with practical applications rapidly developing in many different areas. There may certainly be unintended consequences as well as legal and ethical issues, but we will learn. And we will learn how to work with machines that learn. Not far into the future a breakthrough innovation may be created by a machine. In such environments, innovation professionals will not be out of work but will have more freedom to choose what they want to do in the creative process.

Accidental discoveries will always occur and new ideas will keep emerging from the minds of visionaries and dreamers. But the majority of innovations come from a dedicated effort to spot and pursue opportunities. They come from the determination and hard work by inventors and entrepreneurs. They come from the ingenuity of individuals and from team collaborations. One idea spawns another. One innovation paves the way for another. And that's how the future is shaped.

Innovation management guru Henry Chesbrough once commented that the last word on innovation may never be written. Innovation is far too complex and dynamic. He may be right, but for an author it's not just about writing. It's just as much about being read and the joy of sharing one's thoughts and ideas with others. And about the satisfaction of knowing that in some way you may have contributed to their success.

Gothenburg in July 2018

Anders Hemre

PREFACE

The idea of innovation appears to be firmly lodged in the human mind. Our need to explore, discover, decorate, dominate, conquer, protect, invent, tell stories and make magic seems to go all the way back to our origin as a species.

The urge to innovate has made us come a long way — from rock carvings to computer art, from rain dances to weather satellites and from smoke signals to smart phones.

Ingenuity and effort, curiosity and collaboration, organization and risk taking, imagination and determination have all helped drive economic, social and technological development in society. No wonder much has been said and much has been written about innovation.

So why write another book about the subject? As for myself, I have lived innovation, I'm passionately interested in it and I like to write. So here it is — another book about innovation.

But this book is special — it's my book. Behind it lie years of practice in new product development, countless discussions with experienced professionals and a great deal of private research. Some content has been previously published in newsletters and print magazines or has been presented at international conferences. Much comes from the Brainovation® blog.

I have largely kept the blogging style, making this less of a traditional text book and more a collection of relatively self contained reflections on the topic of the book title — The Creative Company.

Here and there I quote the views of others to avoid complete self centricity. Hopefully that has contributed to a better book than otherwise would have been the case. But, as a dabbling cartoonist, I could not resist the temptation to include a few samples of my own creative work.

This book — the first in a series of three about modern management — wants to promote the art of working with ideas and inspire organizations to find new and better ways of becoming more creative and better manage innovation. I have certainly enjoyed writing it. I hope you will enjoy reading it.

Gothenburg in April 2014

Anders Hemre

THE CASE FOR INNOVATION

"You see things that are and say why,
but I dream things that never were
and say why not"
George Bernard Shaw

Everybody agrees — innovation is good. It solves problems and makes breakthroughs happen. It transforms industries, creates new markets and contributes to economic growth. It changes ways of life. And yet, quite often it also fails.

"Innovation is outside the comfort zones of most businesses, but so is bankruptcy."
- Aaron Shapiro

In itself, innovation is complex and multifaceted. It is a concept, a phenomenon, a strategy, a business process, an engine for growth and a source of competitive strength. It can be looked at from a range of perspectives — all the way from the global economy to the creativity of individuals. It lends itself to research, consulting, book writing, academic courses, workshops and conference topic. You hear the word a lot in government agencies, corporate offices and boardrooms.

It attracts plenty of venture capital. It generates a lot of buzz and well over one **billion** hits on Google.

Management gurus make a living from it.

But first and foremost innovation is something you *do*. And even if *you* don't — or don't do it well enough — somebody else certainly will. Consequences could be severe. As digital agency executive Aaron Shapiro has pointed out, *"innovation is outside the comfort zones of most businesses, but so is bankruptcy."*

Innovation should be the easy choice then. Sure, but wait a minute…

Early, weak or ambiguous signals are difficult to act on. Risk aversion and business blind spots lead to missed opportunities and competitive failures. Too many good ideas end up not making it through the development funnel even if in retrospect they should have and companies often look at markets through the lenses of their current business. Clearly, with innovation comes great opportunity as well as considerable challenge.

But despite difficulties and hurdles few people consider innovation something that shouldn't be pursued. On the contrary, economic policy makers, business leaders and company managers all promote innovation and countless individuals worldwide make their contributions to innovation as inventors, entrepreneurs and practitioners in research, new product and service development, architecture, industrial design and other professional fields. A great deal of experience has thus been gained over time, but the environment in which innovation happens has also become more complex and challenging making it more difficult — and more important — to get it right. There may simply be little time and few opportunities for a second or third attempt. Still, companies need to keep looking for innovation opportunities. And they need to look in three directions.

When companies look forward, they not only try to imagine the possibilities of the future, but they also build confidence in the face of uncertainty and stimulate more creative contributions.

When companies look around themselves, they may see new needs and growing incongruities and may find new ways to create value through existing or emerging technologies.

When companies look deeply at themselves, they may find new ways of being innovative and making breakthroughs happen.

In doing so, it is not the need to innovate that is new. It's rather the rate and precision at which innovation must happen that is of prime concern. At the same time, innovation is driven not just by the pursuit of profit or market dominance, but just as much by the innate human wish to explore, understand and improve. Innovation is thus to a large extent a people centric process. And as such it starts with something quite fundamental — the creativity and curiosity of the human mind.

UNDERSTANDING CREATIVITY

"I start with an idea
and then it turns into something else"
Pablo Picasso

The words of the 20th century Spanish painter and co-inventor of cubism say a great deal about the creative process not only in the arts but in many other fields as well. The creative process is unpredictable, non-deterministic and difficult to manage. Yet, as a key ingredient in innovation, creativity must be understood, nurtured and exploited. The good news is that creative thinking is a skill and as such it can be learned.

And learning is a matter of the mind.

1 MIND MATTERS

In a way human thinking is not very deep. In fact, one could argue it's only a couple of millimeters deep. That's the thickness of the human brain's cortex or outer layer of grey matter. It contains some 20 billion neurons — about four times that of a chimpanzee and five thousand times that of a mouse.
Thinking capacity comes not only from the number of neurons though, but more importantly from the number of neuron connections.

With individual neurons typically having thousands of connections to other neurons, the neural network of a human brain is enormously complex and also unique to each individual.

Somewhat simplified, the brain's mechanism for thinking consists of neurons moving electrical impulses around in large and complex networks with special neurotransmitters bridging synaptic gaps. It's all in the network as individual neurons only serve as relay stations, receiving inputs that may or may not trigger an electrical action potential that is passed on to other neurons, which simply repeat the process.

It's this bio-electrochemical mechanism that is behind not only our sensory perceptions but in fact all our ideas, thoughts and dreams. It's how we are able to think — through a massive collaboration of neurons.

Despite advances in medical technology such as functional magnetic resonance imaging (fMRI), detailed study of the brain's neural activity is very difficult. Completely mapping the brain's connectivity — the human *"connectome"* — is much more difficult than mapping the human genome. Add the mind and things get even more difficult.

Some researchers have gone as far as suggesting that mind and consciousness have something to do with a complex phenomenon of quantum mechanics — entanglement.

Be that as it may, for now we have to accept that the basic mystery remains: how the brain relates to the mind — and the mind to the brain.

However, there is no doubt we are thinking. Triggering centuries of discussions, French philosopher René Descartes made the famous suggestion *"I think, therefore I am"*, reversing the more obvious *"I am, therefore I think"*.

Descartes' simple play with words is a good example of stimulating creativity and deep thinking, not unlike the koans or riddles used in Zen Buddhism, albeit in that case for a different purpose.

Thinking is a cognitive process. As such it can be done more or less well and it can create a wide range of outcomes from brilliant insights to the wrong conclusions and even to acts of great foolishness. And strict logic can lead astray if the starting point of the analysis is wrong.

One could argue there are basically three kinds of thinking — analytical, creative and emotional, corresponding to our deliberate, opportunistic and automatic brain systems. All three are involved in innovation.

New ideas emerge from creative thinking and are being accepted or rejected under the influence of not only logical analysis but also a number of human psychological and emotional factors.

Risk aversion may have saved companies from making some bad investments, but is also responsible for many failures to pursue great opportunities.

Mental models are necessary for sense making, but may also lead to rejection of ideas that don't fit.

Anchoring — the mind's preference for starting new thinking from the last previous thought — not only results in linear thinking, but can also lead to gross errors in making "gut feel" estimates.

Nevertheless, creative thinking does occur and thinking "straight" happens also in a non-linear world.
In line with the great engineering definition of time — "time is what clocks measure" — creative thinking could simply be described as the kind of thinking that leads to creative outcomes.
To make it more interesting, such outcomes may have originated in the famous *eureka moment* — a sudden and illuminating insight.

2 THE EUREKA MOMENT

Serendipity and sudden insight lie behind many well known creative breakthroughs, including e.g. Otto Loewi's dream triggered discovery of the chemical nature of nerve impulses. Other eureka triggered breakthroughs include Velcro, Post-its, the microwave oven, the bar code and plenty of others. And no doubt many more will come.

What is it that happens in the brain when an insight occurs?
19th century microbiologist Louis Pasteur once said, *"Chance favors the prepared mind"*. He probably said it in French, but modern neuroscience still tends to agree.
It goes something like this. We're looking for a solution to a challenging problem and the brain starts working — more specifically the analytical engine of the left brain. It's when we cannot solve a problem despite thinking hard about it that things may get interesting. Exhausting the analytical capacity and reaching an impasse followed by relaxing, sleeping or doing something different seems to somehow activate the creative engine of the right brain opening new pathways in subsidiary awareness.

Orchestrated by the prefrontal cortex, it seems like the priming of the left brain followed by decreased activity shifts the responsibility for problem solving over to the right brain, which starts probing the synaptic network for promising connections.

When neurons fire in a new pattern that represents the solution and this is brought into awareness, an insight occurs. In this way, the brain makes new combinations of fragments or chunks of knowledge to form new ideas and make creative breakthroughs.
We experience such a type of insight as sudden, certain and satisfactory. The reason it doesn't happen all the time is that Pasteur was right. The mind needs a good problem to work on and it needs to be well prepared when chance presents the opportunity.

3 BETTER BOXES

I was thinking outside the box — Too bad it was the wrong box

© Anders Hemre

Entrepreneur, author and humanitarian Dan Pallotta once wrote *"you cannot possibly think outside the box unless you understand the nature of the box that bounds your current thinking"*. Perhaps so, but then again one might wonder if creativity is really concerned about the nature of the box.

It's true that while reframing an issue or when looking at a problem from a new perspective it may be helpful to be aware of what bounds your current thinking. But when a truly creative breakthrough occurs, it's often the result of hard thinking *inside* the box followed by no thinking — or thinking about something different — that prepares the brain for a new and creative approach rather than deliberately thinking about the box and trying to get out of it.

With reference to the highly structured compositions created by famous painters such as Piet Mondrian and Paul Klee, psychologist Patricia D. Stokes suggests that creativity can actually be stimulated by being constrained. Paradoxically, rules and restrictions appear to enhance imaginative thinking. Stokes also uses the meticulous and disciplined practice of French impressionist master Claude Monet as an illustration of how constraint fuels creativity.

Whether thinking in art or business, there is always a box and boundaries don't really disappear. But we can perhaps poke a hole in the box or move the boundaries and think in bigger boxes. We can think in more or better boxes.

And we can think together.

4 THINKING TOGETHER

Creativity is commonly viewed as a purely individual trait, primarily because it's associated with cognitive and neurophysiologic processes in the (individual) human brain. In other words, moments of creative insight occur in individuals but not in teams.

This view is lingering, but in recent years, research on creativity has been broadened. Cross-disciplinary efforts involving social psychologists, organizational behaviorists and even economists have led to an increased recognition of the importance of social factors.

It's been argued that if a company wants to be more creative, the best thing it can do is to hire some creative people. It could also be the worst thing to do, if the organizational environment is not really conducive to creative contributions. The new creative hires will soon find out, switch their minds off or head for the exit.

There are, however, things companies can do to stimulate creativity and increase their return on creative effort. Organizing idea competitions and brain-storming sessions can certainly be helpful, but return on creativity also requires a continuous capacity.

A logical (yes, left brain) analysis would go something like this. The more creative people an organization has and the more creative and motivated these people are, the more creative the company. Creativity would thus be viewed as an individual capacity that can more or less be added up as "creativity headcount".

From another perspective, one could argue that social networks, knowledge and idea exchanges and overall communication and collaboration could stimulate and strengthen creative contributions.

Therefore organization, culture and work practices — although not themselves creative — help define creative capacity. We have plenty of dots (i.e. creative people) and we connect them. Engaged and motivated creative minds "wired" together form a creative organization.

5 BEING CREATIVE

Can you measure creativity?
Several models for doing so have been proposed, funny enough including both CAT (Consensual Assessment Technique) and RAT (Remote Associates Test). However, and not too surprisingly, creativity measurements have not been widely used in organizations. Partly because of the nature of the subject, but also because organizations — and their managers — prefer to *do* things more than develop a deep understanding of things.
Some of the latter may be useful though. According to Harvard researcher Teresa Amabile, creativity expresses itself through a combination of expertise (creative) thinking and motivation. The latter is a key factor that is often overlooked.

Extrinsic motivation is closely related to management and incentives. Too much may be perceived as coercion and too little as lack of interest.

Intrinsic motivation is different in nature and can be difficult to work with, but it needs to be understood. Good managers know what really motivates people. And good managers find ways to work with *organizational slack* — another key factor in promoting creativity and innovation.

Intrinsic motivation, continuity and positive feelings are known to stimulate creativity. However, idea management has traditionally been approached mainly through process and technology, where a fair amount of knowledge and experience has been gained. The people side of the ideation performance equation has not developed to the same level of understanding and managers are generally not very well equipped to address human and organizational issues in the "front end of the front end" of innovation.

Intrinsic motivations may differ between individuals, but organizations tend to also develop a shared set of attitudes and behaviors relating to ideation. That's why companies can adopt a common approach to idea work and deliberately seek creative breakthroughs.

6 MAKING BREAKTHROUGHS HAPPEN

Some innovation gurus advise against idea generation getting into creative over-gear, coming up with crazy ideas or far-fetched solutions looking for a problem. Fair enough. But looking at innovation as a business practice, one should try to maintain a few small practice areas that involve really creative thinking. Not only would these serve as idea generators, but also as "workout" places where people could learn creative thinking and problem solving techniques. There have been suggestions we could call such creative practice areas *ideation cells* or maybe *creation cells*. But of course it's not about what they're called. And it's not about beanbag chairs, pink office walls and music at work. It's about the kind of thinking that goes on — creative thinking, for creative outcomes.

New ideas come with both risk and uncertainty. These are not the same. Risk can be managed, but not uncertainty. The latter can be modeled though, e.g. using the four uncertainty levels suggested by Hugh Courtney for future scenarios — one future, alternative futures, a range of possibilities and full ambiguity.
In fact, uncertainty brings opportunity. Uncertainty thus has value and is in itself also a strong driver of creative thinking.

Many techniques have been tried to avoid getting stuck in the dreaded analytical, linear thinking. Examples include reframing, combining and connecting, doodling, random words, six thinking hats and mind mapping.
Creativity enhancing tools could be of some value, but won't replace the brainwork required. After all, we think with our minds and not with technology.

Actually, two of the more useful techniques are quite simple to apply — eliminating a given component from an existing or proposed design to force a search for different alternatives and introducing a seemingly unrelated concept or object to suggest an entirely new perspective on a problem or opportunity.

> *"Creative breakthroughs come when they're ready and not on command."*

No tool or technique may be perfect and every attempt at facilitating creative thinking might not succeed. To avoid ending up with just low hanging fruit, even brainstorming sessions could be repeated several times around the same topic to generate more and better ideas.

Creative breakthroughs will come, but they come when they're ready and not on command. Being creative takes time.

7 TIME TO THINK

We need to save time

Yes, but not now. I'm on my coffee break

© Anders Hemre

"The more time pressure people feel on a given day, the less likely they will be to think creatively" wrote Teresa Amabile over a decade ago. Drop the word "creatively" and the remark would still be true. One could argue that an organization that does not allow itself time to think, may turn into a thoughtless organization.

Even if a new insight occurs in a sudden moment, it doesn't mean that creative thinking as such occurs in a flash. Thinking takes time. And creative thinking takes time too. In today's high paced work environments with frequent interruptions and information overload, the situation is even more challenging than when Amabile first made her observation.

Managers often assume that if there is no time today for innovative play, there will always be time tomorrow. Maybe, but it's not all about time. It's also about inspiration, motivation and about trust in leadership and confidence in the future. And it's about access to information and connectivity to others.

Making room for creative contributions thus involves quite a bit more than just having time. And then there needs to be a good problem to work on — for one mind or more. Perhaps even during coffee breaks.

8 STORM OR BREEZE

First introduced by Alex F. Osborn well over half a century ago, brainstorming has enjoyed a surprisingly long life. Way beyond the life span of most faddy concepts. One reason might be that it's a simple concept with a cute label easy to market. And Osborn was actually an advertising executive.

Over the years, many brainstorms have created good ideas. But many have also produced rather mediocre results.

Most likely traditional brainstorming is somewhat past its prime. With advances in cognitive psychology and neuroscience, brainstorming has come under increased suspicion of being not all that effective in storming up really great ideas. One obvious reason is that groups have a tendency for group think.

Neuroscientist Jonah Lehrer has gone as far as claiming that there is one main problem with group brainstorming — it doesn't work. If Lehrer is right, "brainbreezing", i.e. individual creative thinking, ongoing smart conversation and pooling ideas for collaboration may be just as good or even better.

The good news is that all organizations need to do is try both ways and see for themselves what works best — storm or breeze.

9 MORE IS MORE. MAYBE

More is certainly more. But is it better?

Just like more eyes see more, more minds think more. But just like thinking alone requires individual thinking skills, collaborative thinking requires collaborative thinking skills. And collaborative thinking is by no means a replacement for thinking alone.

In fact, while thinking in groups engages more minds and thus more knowledge and more creativity, it also creates more diversions, more distractions and more interruptions. And it introduces social dynamics. Still, with sufficient preparation and follow up and with experienced people and skilled facilitators involved one could generally expect good outcomes from thinking in groups.

"Just as more minds think more,
better minds think better."

On the other hand, both creative and deep thinkers are often highly individualistic and need private space. The lone genius is not dead. Not by a long shot.

Research by neuroscientist Kenneth Kishida and others shows that when people solve problems in small groups, they may lose some of their cognitive capacity compared with when doing it alone.

Social interaction, perception of status and other factors seem to interfere with the cognitive processes involved in problem solving. That may not be so surprising. We've all heard of — and probably experienced — a number of cognitive phenomena such as group think, halo effect, anchoring and others.

So, once again, research has shown that we are not as sharp thinkers as we might want to believe — at least not all the time.

10 CONSTRAINING CREATIVITY

Creativity is an innate capability of humans. In organizations, there need to be conditions for this capability to engage and express itself, i.e. there need to be conditions for people to make — and want to make — creative contributions. On the opposite, the lack or absence of such conditions puts a constraint on creativity in organizations. Here are three contenders to look out for:

- Lack of confidence
- Lack of time
- Lack of structure

Confidence in the future stimulates creative contributions. Therefore lack of confidence in the strategies and leadership of an enterprise has the opposite effect. It could perhaps in some cases lead to innovative skunk work, but in general and as the result of reduced intrinsic motivation, it tends to limit the number and quality of contributions that people volunteer.

Enterprises aspiring to be creative need to find ways to operate with some degree of organizational slack, i.e. time for people to contribute above and beyond current assignments.
Another way organizations often engineer lack of time into their operation is the application of arbitrary deadlines. These are deadlines imposed for the sole purpose of putting pressure on individuals and teams — a way for managers to make their contribution. Of course organizations should be focused and hard working people get things done. But continuously operating this way has some ramifications. Not only does it reduce or eliminate organizational slack, it may also take away the very incentive to be creative and the room to make any contributions beyond what's obviously expected.

Lack of structure as a constraining factor may seem somewhat counterintuitive. And indeed, in some organizations a "free form" environment may stimulate creativity. But in most organizations, making room for creative contributions would benefit from a well formulated challenge and from some designated roles, a place to go with new ideas and a way to orchestrate a productive interplay between creativity, management and expertise. It would increase the return on creativity. It may even bring about that big idea

11 WHAT'S THE BIG IDEA?

OK, you have a good idea. It could be a big one, it could be a small one or it could be one that just needs to bake a little more. Now what? Well, next you could:

- Imagine the outcome
- Craft the message
- Evolve the concept
- Evaluate the opportunity
- Build the alliance
- Expand the view
- Do the numbers
- Make the case
- Choose the path
- Lead the way

The point is that even a good idea needs some work before it's ready to roll. And rolling a new idea uphill can be hard work, even if it's a good one. But within a good idea may grow the seeds of even better ones, making hard work pay off beyond the initial return.

Not all ideas are good ideas. Some ideas *are* bad — or at least not so good. So what should be done with bad ideas? The most obvious answer is to discard them. After all, why would anyone want to pursue a bad idea?
Why indeed, but even a bad idea may be worth some attention before it's tossed in the shredder. After all, it was probably conceived with a good intention. Despite being a bad idea, it probably addressed a real problem or

pointed to a potential opportunity. If so, the conception of a bad idea could thus trigger the search for a better one.

12 ENTREPRENEURIAL INNOVATION

In addition to the high profile innovations we have come to expect in areas such as consumer electronics, ICT and life sciences, there is also a great deal of good old entrepreneurial innovation still around, often in industries that we don't normally think of as highly innovative.

What such innovations pretty much have in common is a clear and concrete problem to solve followed by a strong entrepreneurial effort resulting in a growing business.

These entrepreneurs probably never read a book about innovation management, never went to an innovation conference and never met an innovation guru. They didn't think about dominant designs, open innovation or prediction markets. They saw a problem and they worked hard to solve it. Then they worked even harder to sell the solution. That's entrepreneurial innovation.

Innovation is often associated with creativity and entrepreneurship with hard work. It seems that innovative entrepreneurs are taking on a double challenge — both creativity and hard work. Not only do they need a box to think outside and some dots to connect.

Even with a great idea, they also need to beat the odds that are stacked against them and clear the hurdles in front of them.

"Most entrepreneurs don't need innovation theory. They need cash."

Innovation theory is good, but most entrepreneurs don't need it. What they need is cash. That doesn't mean that it is money that will make them successful. But money will make it possible for entrepreneurs to take their idea — and themselves — to the test. Like author and entrepreneurship guru Guy Kawasaki suggests, a chance to *make meaning first*.

It goes without saying that entrepreneurs believe in what they are trying to do. Kawasaki goes as far as suggesting that pitches to venture capitalists should not claim "a proven team", refer to market research by the big firms or claim that estimates are conservative. That's what everybody does and VC people don't pay that much attention to it. But they do want to feel the power of an idea and understand the meaning it makes.

In the end though, making meaning and having a burning desire to turn an idea into reality cannot replace, but must complement, answers to the inevitable questions: what does it take, what will it cost, who will fund it and what's the return?

13 GUIDED IDEATION

In organizations, ideas are intangible assets. As such they should be subject to some form of intangible asset management — in this case idea management or *guided ideation*.

The purpose of a guided ideation process is to increase the return on creativity in organizations in support of both innovation and problem solving. This may involve a number of key objectives and challenges such as stimulating creativity, generating and capturing ideas, engaging relevant expertise and valuating new concepts.
The successful implementation of a guided ideation process should result in both organizational and business benefits.

These would include

- Adding structure, definition and visibility to the early stage of innovation
- Providing ideation language and vocabulary
- Adding consistency in creating, developing and evaluating new ideas
- Increasing the level of innovation (more good ideas) and accelerating learning
- Increasing the return on innovation

Over time, R&D and Engineering organizations develop strong expertise in technology and in product development processes. They also typically show a preference for analytical (versus creative) thinking. Even though such expertise and skills are necessary in technological innovation, it does not automatically follow that experienced and competent organizations are also highly creative. However, creativity *can* be developed and creative thinking *can* be learned.

Creativity research suggests both process (ideation) and management (guidance) as well as intrinsic motivation play key roles in driving creativity and innovation in organizations.

Working on interesting technology is certainly a key intrinsic motivator in R&D organizations. It is, however, not the only one.
Creativity is closely related to positive emotions and perceptions of progress. On the other hand, a strong focus on performance and efficiency — important as these may be — can be difficult to reconcile with a need for creativity and innovation.

Creativity, to be useful, requires both convergent and divergent thinking and both individual thinking and thinking in teams. Even though creativity can be stimulated, it has some limitations. Technology and product areas to some extent determine the creative potential (i.e., it's not just about the people) and creative ideas to a large extent originate from what individuals are actually working on (i.e., what they naturally think about). This implies that the driving context for ideation is constructed both from the characteristics of technologies and products, people's knowledge and perception of these as well as from the innate creativity and curiosity of the human mind.
Ideas may emerge spontaneously or as a result of organized efforts. In both cases they need to be captured.

Ideas that remain tacit (i.e. as cognitive entities in the minds of people) can only be expressed by engaging people in idea collaborations, reviews and discussions. Ideas expressed in explicit form can, of course, be captured more easily and submitted to an idea repository.

It is not only the initial idea conception that is important. The subsequent discussions, comments, reviews, enhancements and collaborations add perspectives and insights that may be necessary to move an idea forward and make it grow into a strong new product concept. Therefore, creating and maintaining a collaborative environment for evolving ideas is crucial to successful ideation. This also helps level the playing field so that ideas can compete on fair terms.

Overall, it is easy to see that the process of ideation is one that, while driven by purpose, needs to be guided rather than managed.

Not everyone can be expected to genuinely care about the organization for which they work (and vice versa).

In R&D environments, this can be particularly noticeable as many professional engineers feel as strong identification with their discipline as they do with their (current) employer. In fact, the smartest and most creative individuals are often the first to disengage if they perceive things are not going the right way. It may even be possible that some individuals feel it more useful keeping a great idea to themselves in case they are laid off or decide to quit. This attitude is obviously not desirable but certainly understandable considering that even rejected ideas are in most cases still legally owned by the company and not by the employee.

Basic human behavior aside, overall — as innovation is forward looking in nature — it is critical that the organization has confidence in the vision and strategies of its leadership. Another important ideation challenge is the often chronic condition of real or perceived lack of time. Both deadlines and everyday distractions take away time necessary for people to make creative contributions.

Ideas need time to "breathe" and people need time to "soak" in the problem, challenge or opportunity. This requires some form of organizational slack or opportunities for people to spend time thinking and connecting with others beyond the needs of their current assignment.

It should be noted that time is required for several different ideation activities: creative thinking, making idea contributions, collaborating with others, participating in events, reviewing contributions and so forth.

Poor definition of problems, challenges and opportunities may also render ideation efforts ineffective. This requires special attention as the urge is often to move quickly towards solutions even if the problem or opportunity has not been that well defined.

It must also be easy for people to make contributions without necessarily having to follow documented procedures or climb a steep learning curve of a new tool.

During idea searches and reviews, people would preferably have access to all existing idea artifacts as well as to relevant market and technology research, in addition to competitive intelligence information. It would therefore be beneficial to maintain an integrated tools environment or at least provide easy access to different information environments.

Having made contributions, most people accept the fact that their ideas may be rejected, but they would like to know why. They would like to get feedback in a timely fashion and they would like to see that, if not their own, at least some ideas are actually acted upon.

In some cases it may be an advantage to have an actual ideation point of contact to approach with an idea instead of simply being referred to an online ideation tool. Such a tool may be a good one, and may include ratings and comments by others, but will always remain impersonal and unable to share the passion a person may feel about their idea.

It is also important for people to be able to stay connected with their idea in case it is adopted for further development. This in turn requires both some overall continuity of technology and projects and some organizational flexibility to allow people the freedom to follow their idea and participate in the effort of moving it to market.

There are basically three ways of organizing ideation:

- open "submit anything anytime" environment
- integrated with the product or service development process
- topic focused and time limited: idea campaigns, events, competitions

The first and the last are the most commonly used, with the latter generally producing better results. The second option would represent somewhat of a semi mandatory approach with ideation activities predefined as part of the work process. It is not necessarily intended to change what's in a new product development project but rather to tap into people's minds as they work through a project.

Serious idea contributions may justify serious incentives such as cash rewards similar to those many organizations offer for patents or even stock options in case ideas develop into actual new products and new business. Tangible incentive, however, should not be used at the expense of working with intrinsic motivation as the latter has been shown to be strongly associated with creative contributions. Nor should the reverse apply.

Even with a guided ideation process in place, confidence in the future no doubt has an impact on people's willingness to make voluntary contributions to the business. When people are not sure about the company future, or their own future with the company, even if they do not deliberately deny the company a great idea, creativity and innovation are simply not first and foremost on their minds.

It may be tempting for management to communicate that individuals making idea contributions are particularly valuable to the business, but this could easily turn into a slippery slope. It may be better for management to demonstrate strategic leadership, create a compelling but realistic vision for the future and, most importantly, provide real, tangible support for innovation.

ORCHESTRATING THE CREATIVE EFFORT

"The secret of getting ahead
is getting started"
Mark Twain

While innovation can be viewed as a *phenomenon* involving random events, serendipity and sudden insights, it may — and must — also be viewed as a *process* involving deliberate intent, organized effort and enabling conditions. The creative process involves discovery, learning and change. It cannot be subject to traditional process management. But it can be *orchestrated* and a well orchestrated creative process will generate an innovative outcome.

American experimental composer John Cage suggested *"begin anywhere"* as the starting point for creative effort, thus avoiding the paralyzing lack of an answer to the natural question *"where do I start?"*

Not only can there be different starting points, there can be different paths forward and even different outcomes.

In the creative process, you don't generate a predictable result. You begin from where you are, stick to your intent, orchestrate the effort, follow through and discover the outcome.

14 TO INNOVATE OR NOT

Two capabilities seem to be of particular importance for companies that wish to be truly innovative — the ability to *recognize great ideas* and *see game changing opportunities*. But if an idea is really great, why wouldn't it be recognized? And if a significant new opportunity presents itself, why wouldn't it be vigorously pursued? One reason could be that ideas and opportunities are not initially seen at their full potential and therefore appear too tiny compared with current business.

Another reason for not recognizing breakthrough opportunities might be that most traditional investment cases work best with new core business products and services in existing or slowly developing markets. The reason simply being that more (and more accurate) information is available for estimates.

How then can one develop the two capabilities mentioned above? Initially in two ways: making serious room on the business agenda and finding fair ways to estimate value.

Two hours on the quarterly results and ten minutes on "new stuff" in senior management meetings simply won't cut it. Nor does pure gut feel in lieu of method.

15 EXCUSES, EXCUSES

There are many good reasons to innovate. And there are many good excuses for *not* innovating. Here are some suggestions from Idea Champions' Mitch Ditkoff:

- I don't have the time
- I can't get the funding
- My boss will never go for it
- We won't be able to get it past legal
- I've got too much on my plate
- I'm just not the creative type
- I'm already juggling way too many projects
- I'm too new around here
- No one, besides me, really cares about innovation
- There's too much bureaucracy here to get anything done
- Our customers aren't asking for it
- We're a risk averse culture, always will be
- We don't have an innovation process
- We don't have a culture of innovation
- They don't pay me enough to take on this kind of project
- My career path will be jeopardized if this doesn't fly

It's of course possible to post counter arguments for most of these:

- If we don't make time we won't have a future
- We can't afford not to take the risk

- Through practice we can — and must — change our culture
- We will put innovation firmly on our management agenda and build a coalition for creativity
- We can't compete in the market of tomorrow with the products of today

Even so, innovation leaders obviously have their job cut out for them.

16 INNOVATION LEADERSHIP

The driving force behind innovation is the wish to create and implement something new. To organize and accomplish this is the task of the innovation leader. Innovators and entrepreneurs know they have to find ways to roll their idea uphill and beat the odds stacked against them. Despite the challenges and difficulties involved, some entrepreneurs actually *do* succeed and some companies *are* clearly more innovative than others. Even though luck and circumstance may influence the outcome, human factors such as determination, perseverance and leadership ultimately make the difference.

What then makes an effective innovation leader? To some extent probably the same characteristics that make an effective leader in general. But there are also some circumstances and issues that specifically challenge innovation leaders, requiring them to

- See emerging high value opportunities before others do
- Navigate through ambiguity, uncertainty and real options
- Engage and get key players on board
- Build networks, coalitions and alliances to help evolve the innovation
- Drive the early effort with credibility and confidence

Things change and in innovative ventures failure *is* an option. Effective innovation leaders need to know when to abort a project should the business case be compromised or a better solution emerge.

More than just killing an idea, in such a case, the innovation team has gained a valuable experience, honed its skills and will be better equipped to deliver when the next opportunity emerges.

But first it needs to be recognized.

17 SEEING WHAT'S THERE

"A blind spot is an area on the eye's retina where no image is formed. By analogy, we all choose at times to turn a blind eye to aspects of reality which we don't like, don't comprehend or we don't want to see. In business, such behavior results in lower earnings, faltering growth, loss of market position and other signs of deteriorating performance. At times, the consequence is nothing short of a competitive disaster."

So wrote competitive intelligence guru Benjamin Gilad more than twenty years ago. Today the situation is not much different. Even companies with a great vision can't always see clearly.

To survive and mature, good ideas need good support. But if good ideas are good for business, why wouldn't they always be supported? Of course, resource availability and decision makers' individual preferences play important roles, but there are also more subtle mechanisms at work involving how people react to the uncertainty inherently associated with something that hasn't been tried before.

It is well known that many of the same organizations that endorse innovation also routinely reject creative ideas. Attitudes towards risk and uncertainty drive such behavior.

A study published by Cornell University suggests that there is indeed an individual bias against creativity in situations where uncertainty is experienced. It concludes with a suggestion that is well worth considering:

"if people have difficulty gaining acceptance for creative ideas especially when more practical and unoriginal options are readily available, the field of creativity may need to shift its current focus from identifying how to generate more creative ideas to identifying how to help innovative institutions recognize and accept creativity".

"Even companies with a great vision can't always see clearly."

It's wise to learn from past mistakes. And innovation is no exception. Many cases from innovation history tell the same story though. Companies turn down a big innovation and instead choose to concentrate on their core business. And when it's obvious what they should have done, it's too late.

Are managers in such companies particularly shortsighted or incompetent? Probably not, it's just difficult to predict the future success of something new. And just knowing that plenty of mistakes have been made in the past, is not very useful to avoid making another one. What can we do then?

Innovation guru Clayton Christensen suggests using *good theory*, i.e. theory with strong predictive power. Christensen is an academic, but he's probably right.

Every year, somewhere, someone will make a colossal mistake and turn down that next big innovation. It is management's responsibility to make sure it's not them. It would not only rob a good company of a great future, but it would also hand over the opportunity to someone else. And they — if they seize it and if they succeed — will be the ones to write innovation history — and perhaps even become proof of Christensen's good theory.

18 IN THE CRYSTAL BALL

The future ain't what it used to be said Yogi Berra. Maybe he was thinking of the many failed predictions of the future that have been served up over long periods of time by futurologists, experts and ordinary people alike. Berra could have said it ain't easy to remember the future — at least not everything that is being said about it. And that may be just as well as most of it will probably turn out to be wrong.

Recognizing the shortcomings of their own profession, futurologists often point out that there is no adequate language for describing the future. Still, using the language of today, scenario planning frequently takes place in companies that are concerned about the future.

Scenarios are exercises in creative and strategic thinking and in the best case outcomes include both accelerated learning and some eureka moments.

For entrepreneurs and innovators, trying to forecast the future or map out different scenarios is not what's most important though. The questions that need to be answered are instead about the present — *what's happening* and *why is it happening now?*

Established firms need to ask the same questions or they risk being the first to not see it coming.

19 FUZZING UP AND FAILING WELL

The front end *is* fuzzy. It's right there where fuzzy — but potentially great — ideas thrive. Innovative organizations know that and they keep the front end fuzzy, while experimenting, learning and maybe even playing. Fuzz is fun.

You don't really want to "unfuzz" the front end. Just find ways to let those ideas or hunches gently roll on to firmer ground, where you can take a closer look at them. Like finding stuff on the beach washed up from the ocean. You may even want to push some emerging ideas back into the fuzz for a while to see what might happen to them. Some ideas make other ideas stick to them and turn into idea clusters with potentially greater value. There is a case for keeping the front-end fuzzed up.

Business history shows that, despite their muscle and might, time and again large companies have been left in the dust by smaller and nimbler ones who seem to "just do it" and get it right.
Based on new ideas, new startups are launched every day. Some will succeed and some will not.

Small companies may not survive an innovation failure. Bigger companies may have enough resources to recover from one or they can downsize, but they too must learn from the experience.

What we hear and read about most of the time are breakthroughs, turnarounds, rapid growth and other business successes. Clearly, both failure and success bring learning opportunities. But to capitalize on such opportunities may not be as straightforward as it appears.
Failure is a complex phenomenon involving uncertainties, decisions, actions and circumstances as well as mental traps and cognitive constraints such as attribution or outcome bias, which may lead to errors in judgment. Such errors don't always lead to bad results and can thus be masked by good outcomes.

Not learning from success can happen e.g. when an organization repeats a successful project architecture without having made assumptions explicit and without knowing exactly why things went well, only to fail when previous success factors have changed or are no longer present.

20 THE INNOVATION DILEMMA

Individual firms need to protect and grow existing business *and* innovate to build future business.

The *innovation dilemma* comes from the simple fact that it is always easier to make the case for continuous improvement of existing products and services than for disruptive technologies and discontinuous innovation.

Latent needs, requirements for future products and services and emerging market and technology developments are present as largely tacit knowledge inside and outside the firm.

Leading innovation occurs when firms are able to turn this emerging, tacit knowledge into new products and services and successfully bring these to market ahead of competition. This is not particularly easy and that in turn is why only a few firms can truly call themselves leading innovators.

Firms that do well in innovation are usually externally focused, have a strong sense of history and concern about the future, exhibit a learning culture and have a high risk tolerance.

Firms that do less well are typically more internally focused, emphasize efficiency, promote a teaching culture and demonstrate low risk tolerance.

The overall innovation management architecture used can obviously make a significant difference.

And there are several to choose from:

- In-house, centralized/dedicated (corporate R&D)
- In-house, distributed/dedicated
- In-house, distributed/not dedicated (open, internal)
- Spin in (innovation cell)
- Spin out (sponsored start-up)
- Co-innovation (open, external, cluster)
- Acquisition (company, technology)
- Outsourced (design house)
- Offshore innovation

There are different challenges involved and firms need to ask themselves how to best manage innovation with the architecture they choose.

And figure out whose job it is.

21 INNOVATION — WHOSE JOB IS IT?

It's easy to agree that quality is everyone's job. Whatever is being done, it should be done right. Most things though in organizations are not everyone's job. That goes for innovation as well. Sure, anyone could have a great idea and there needs to be a way to capture and seriously evaluate ideas wherever they come from, but that's not the same thing as innovation being everyone's job.

But it has to be *someone's* job. Or rather the job of a small group of creative and well connected people with a mandate and who can inspire others, help ideas evolve and get traction, draw in expertise and get management involved. The latter can be tricky and managers can be hard to convince when ideas come with uncertainty and risk.

There can certainly be concerns about the business potential of a new idea. What should *not* be an innovation concern, however, is whether a new product will work. If it's built, it will. After all, isn't quality everyone's job?

> *"Innovation is not everyone's job.*
> *But it has to be someone's job."*

If innovation is everyone's job, large companies would be extremely innovative. We know they're not and there is a reason why. It's not just because they're large. It could be argued that it's not actually their job to innovate.

Medium to large companies primarily need to preserve, protect and grow their existing business. Of course they also need to improve products and services and innovate in their core business. Most do and some even run idea campaigns and business plan competitions or make acquisitions of small, innovative companies all in an effort to be more competitive, grow faster or gain market share.

But really creative and potentially game changing innovation will probably continue to come from unknowns in the left field and when least expected. Some of these entrepreneurial ventures will fail and others will be acquired. A few will go on to become large and less innovative companies themselves. And that's ok.

The left field will still be there.

22 OPENING UP

Open innovation has been well researched and practiced for quite some time now. It's about making R&D borders more porous and reaching beyond the boundaries of the firm for new ideas and technologies.

There may be two important implications. One is the obvious need to manage innovation in an open environment. The other may be less obvious, but as the open innovation model creates more opportunities through technology, it becomes increasingly important to analyze and understand market and business aspects.

To some extent traditional market research gets replaced by the "market laboratories" created by venture capital and start-up companies. It therefore becomes important for established firms to closely monitor what goes on in new technology ventures not only to identify potential acquisition targets or licensing opportunities, but also to accelerate learning, observe early market responses and develop sound business models.

There is a fair number of trendy concepts to choose from such as co-innovation, creation-nets, crowd sourcing and others. BT and Proctor & Gamble are examples of large firms that have turned to open innovation models. From a pure knowledge and idea point of view, it is easy to see that firms can benefit from tapping into external sources. The issue is therefore not so much whether to network or not, but rather to establish a networking strategy and figure out how value will be created. Inevitably, there will be issues involving intellectual property rights, commercialization and appropriation of gains.

A new breed of business entities — innovation brokers — has been established to facilitate open innovation. Examples include *NineSigma*, *InnoCentive* and *Presans*.

Open call, crowd-sourcing and crowd-funding have become important ways of reaching out to external organizations, experts and investors.

Using these types of intermediaries and resources may not be for everyone, but firms relying on the development of new products and services are well advised to at least investigate the concept before they develop a strategy for innovation.

Open innovation may appear as a business choice that firms make based on assessing their own innovation capability in view of strategy and objectives. This may of course be the case, but there may also be more fundamental reasons involved for a shift towards open innovation.

In either case, dividing innovative tasks in the fuzzy front-end across firm boundaries will make things more interesting — and more challenging.

23 THE FUZZY, THE MESSY AND THE MURKY

How do you manage a messy process that starts with a fuzzy front end trying to address a murky market? Possibly not very well — at least if applying traditional management methods.

So how *do* you manage innovation?
A guiding principle for building innovation systems is the orchestrated interaction and productive interplay between *creativity, expertise* and *management.*
The same can be used as the starting point for assessing the effectiveness and performance of an established innovation system.
Clearly, looking at all three actors involved, a system of innovation may appear complex. The role of creativity in e.g. the arts is well understood, but it may be less clear how creativity makes its contribution in business.
In addition, while negotiating the complexity of building and operating a system of innovation, one can hardly escape Drucker's cleverly crafted key management question: *what needs to be accomplished?* Without expected outcomes articulated it is difficult to judge the effectiveness of any design, including the design of an innovation system.

In R&D it may be taken for granted that creativity, expertise and management naturally combine in new product development. To some extent they do, but designing an effective system of innovation in R&D organizations still involves a range of unique issues and challenges.

Today, with the ever increasing speed of change and with greater complexity and business uncertainty, it is not picking one particular method that will do the job *even if an organization learns the method well.* Nor should one just go with the (chaotic) flow.
Understanding multiple methods and applying them when and where they make sense would be a better approach to managing the early stage of innovation.
Or maybe it's not as much managing as guiding and making room for exploration, discovery and learning. Surprisingly, a "messy process" can bring both purpose and structure to the fuzzy front end of innovation. A good example is campaigning for ideas.

24 IDEA CAMPAIGNS

> How did the idea campaign go?
>
> We got three good and three bad ideas. That evened it out, so we don't need to do anything

Even though an open and asynchronous ideation process ("submit anything anytime") makes it convenient to contribute, it does not create compelling reasons to do so. An ideation process organized as a series of idea campaigns would most likely yield a better overall result.

Idea campaigns are organized innovation challenges with relatively short time durations and focused on predetermined business opportunities or technology problems. Typically two campaign sessions could be launched on the same topic to reach an appropriate number of people, thereby also allowing the second session to build on the results of the first.

Not all idea campaigns lead to successful innovations. During the 2010 Gulf of Mexico oil disaster, BP invited members of the public to submit ideas for sealing off the leaking well and for cleaning up. Despite receiving over 120,000 ideas from more than 100 countries, the responses did not lead to anything significant.

Other high profile attempts have resulted in similar experiences.

But there are also many examples of successful idea campaigns. Well-articulated innovation challenges motivate creative thinking and facilitate collaborative ideation. As contributions would cluster in the targeted area, an idea evaluation may be performed in bulk by a single team of experts and managers, making the review cycle more efficient.

Idea campaigns are useful in that they serve as the "front end" of ideation helping to communicate importance, raise urgency and focus the creative effort in time and on particular challenges. They also demonstrate management commitment and could thereby make it easier for people to make time for idea contributions. Most likely it will also be easier to find an internal sponsor willing to invest in ideas that result from campaigns organized and promoted by management.

The ideation process could be greatly facilitated by designating organizational roles. This also demonstrates management support and such roles could include *ideation guide*, *idea campaign manager* and *idea champion*.

In conjunction with idea campaigns a review team could be designated to secure the availability of sufficient time and expertise for idea evaluations.

25 IDEATION AND IDEA MANAGEMENT

Ideation and product development are different in nature requiring organizations to maintain — and reconcile — a wide range of skills. The two areas tend to focus on different performance aspects:

- *Entrepreneurial vs Conforming*
- *Creativity vs Performance*
- *Individual knowledge vs Organizational competence*
- *People centric vs Process centric*
- *Learning culture vs Teaching culture*
- *High risk tolerance vs Low risk tolerance*
- *Top line focus vs Bottom line focus*

Ideation performance is determined by a number of intrinsic and contextual factors. Even if less inclusive, a more targeted and focused approach may yield a better result in organizations where ideation relies on voluntary contributions.

From a management perspective there are some easy measures and some more difficult ones. Unfortunately some of the more difficult ones are crucial and unless addressed, the easier measures may not yield the benefits expected.

It is possible to raise the level of creativity and increase the return on innovative effort in organizations, provided that three important factors are addressed: *driving the effort, creating engagement* and *making time*. And again, concerning the latter, management need a way to approach the issue of organizational slack.

There are a surprising number of issues that can occur while deploying a system for ideation:

- Not reaching enough number of people
- Not reaching the right people (people with good ideas they wish to share; domain experts)
- No or insufficient business context for ideation
- No or insufficient (pre-)definition of the business/technology problem to solve
- No (pre-)definition of the business/technology opportunity to pursue

- Lack of process definition/No perception of ideation as a core process or idea management as a key discipline
- Insufficient tools and techniques to support creativity, idea generation, collaboration and knowledge sharing
- Lack of collaboration impacting quantity and quality of ideas
- Lack of diversity in the composition of ideation teams impacting quantity and quality of ideas
- No perception of real importance
- No perception of real urgency
- People actually don't have any good or particularly creative ideas
- People don't feel compelled to engage
- People think their manager will not appreciate them spending time on ideation
- People feel they don't have time to engage
- People are concerned that spending time on ideation shows they are not busy enough
- People feel their ideas will not be taken seriously
- People feel there will not be enough resources allocated to pursue their idea (i.e. no point submitting it)
- People don't feel it's part of their job to submit ideas
- People don't see how they can benefit from contributing ideas
- Ideas are prematurely discarded resulting in missed opportunities
- Weak or ineffective "funneling effort" (reviewing, evaluating, prioritizing, positioning…)
- People feel their ideas may be hijacked or exploited by others (who will then benefit)
- People are afraid their ideas will be rejected, distorted or ridiculed
- People feel that the reward for submitting good or great ideas is nonexistent or not fair
- People feel there may be subtle penalties for submitting "bad" ideas
- People have ideas but just don't want to share them
- People have ideas but don't want to share them publicly
- People have ideas but feel they are too vague to be shared (early self censorship)
- People have ideas and are willing to share them, but are reluctant to use the ideation tool
- People don't want their ideas to be rated in public or rated by peers
- People may feel unsure about criticizing ideas submitted by experts and managers or ideas promoted by senior management

- People feel that the idea rating and evaluation system will be politically manipulated
- Managers may be reluctant to contribute (not because they lack good ideas, but because they are managers)
- Experts may be reluctant to contribute (not because they lack good ideas, but because they are experts)

Obviously, these are not issues that all need to be resolved in conjunction with introducing a system for idea management. They are concerns that could be addressed in case it turns out that ideation performance falls short of expectation in terms of the number or quality of ideas.

There are several commercial tools for managing ideas available to organizations looking for technology support. Most tools offer a range of idea management features such as e.g. idea submissions and search, idea collaboration and support for idea campaigns.

Idea artifacts could be constructed using a standard format including e.g.:

- Originator(s)
- Source (internal/external, campaign, brainstorm…)
- Description
- Information (research, competitive intelligence…)
- Comments and discussions
- Current status (under evaluation, review complete…)
- Reviews and ratings
- Value estimate
- Implementation considerations (technology, cost…)
- Intellectual property considerations

For a complete view of a particular topic and to see how ideas may have clustered, individual idea artifacts could also include references to supporting, competing and opposing ideas.
Collectively, idea artifacts constitute a portfolio of intangible assets. A standard format facilitates idea comparisons as well as the estimation of the portfolio's intellectual capital value.

For organizations that like to measure how they are doing, a well designed idea management tool will be able to provide information also for tracking innovation performance.

26 INNOVATION METRICS

Innovation management surveys repeatedly confirm that many organizations continue to struggle with managing and measuring innovation. Executives typically indicate that the most commonly applied innovation measurements are revenue, profitability and customer satisfaction, none of which are particularly innovation specific.

Of course, some firms have added more innovation specific indicators, adopting a balanced set of innovation metrics covering *input, process* and *output:*

- Number of new ideas
- Business Unit investments in innovation
- R&D % of sales
- Staffing in technical areas
- Idea to decision time
- Decision to launch time
- Project types & launch dates
- Total projected NPV
- Patents granted
- New product launches
- New product sales and profits % of total
- Innovation ROI

One can always argue about individual measures and what actual numbers really mean, but the above provides a decent overall view of innovation.

Overall one can suspect that companies, unless they make a special effort to engineer their metrics for innovation, use what's most easily obtained from their R&D organizations or what's already being tracked by accounting and by customer surveys.

One can also suspect that not so many companies use highly sophisticated metrics or statistical methods in the area of innovation performance — and to some extent rightfully so.

After all, and despite the need for good metrics, it's probably more important to *do* innovation than to measure it.

BUILDING A PATHWAY TO PROFIT

"Even an idea that is bold
is worthless until sold"
Don Snyder

Successful companies don't just innovate — they innovate better. Such companies demonstrate not only the ability to manage the innovation process but to manage it exceptionally well. They may seek market dominance but also effective and productive ways to express the curiosity and creativity of their people.

Some firms engage in a continuous innovation effort. Others innovate when they see a big enough return or when they find themselves under competitive pressure.

In today's fast changing and globally competitive business environment, innovation is no longer a specialty just for start-up companies or industry leaders, but rather a necessity for all.

27 FROM MIND TO MARKET

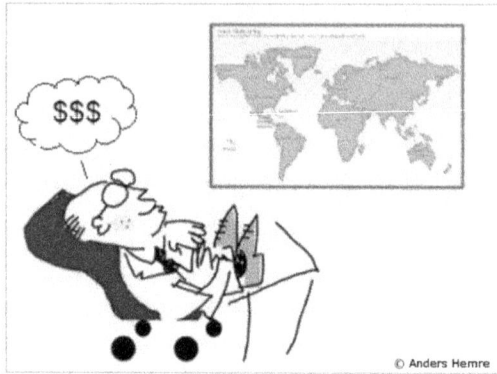

Innovation involves risk and uncertainty and turning tacit knowledge into leading innovation is a significant challenge. Most organizations recognize the value of creativity and the benefit of good ideas. At the same time many organizations still have few, if any, organized ways of managing ideas or securing returns on creative effort. This is particularly obvious when comparing with the often well developed systems for managing technologies and projects once an idea is being pursued for development.

Obviously, ideas that can convert into projects that result in higher revenues and profits would normally be preferred over ideas with less business potential or ideas that would be particularly difficult or costly to implement.

Innovation can be both expensive and uncertain. In some industries, e.g. the airplane and auto manufacturing industries, the cost of innovation can be quite staggering.
To cover their high cost, firms in innovation based industries need to generate above average profit. They also need to maintain their intellectual property rights and overcome trade barriers. And they need large markets. But large markets also sustain more competitors, which is both good and bad. Competition may be of short term benefit to consumers by keeping prices low, but excess competition reduces scale and lowers profit — profit that could have been invested in new innovation, leaving future consumers with less value.

There seems to be a case for more innovation friendly global trade policies. Such policies will not only encourage companies to seek global markets, but also to work harder with the fundamental challenge of managing innovation — being the best they can in going from mind to market.

The following reasons seem to be the most common why a firm may need to increase its innovation effort:

- The firm's growth targets require new products, services or markets
- The portion of the firm's business from new products or services is too small
- The return on new product or service development is insufficient
- The firm is not sufficiently competitive in existing markets and technologies
- The firm is not proactively engaging emerging technologies and markets
- Future scenarios indicate significant threats to the firm's position in the market

There may also be additional conditions indicating or predicting weak performance:

- The firm is losing reputation as a leading innovator
- The firm is losing critical or cutting edge knowledge
- The firm is not attracting new top talent in research & development

If left unaddressed, conditions like the ones above inevitably translate to an innovation gap that can be expressed as a future loss of revenue or putting additional revenues at risk.

E.g. when a company estimates that $r\%$ of total future revenue R must come from new products but innovates at only $c\%$ of full capacity, it would mean that $(100 - c)\% \times r\% \times R$ of future revenue is at risk.
An innovation performance capacity under 100% obviously comes from not doing what should, or what could, be done.

Overall, from the perspective of developing new products and services, it is the moving of innovation from serendipity and accidental discovery towards being a deliberate process that will make the difference in business.
From a management perspective, even though it is not possible to predict the outcome of creative processes, it is certainly possible to create and manage conditions for such processes to execute — and to execute well.
Innovation management is not about saying yes to everything, but new ideas must at least be given a fair chance to compete. To be considered, they need

to clear some initial hurdles and make it across the idea chasm — the organizational behavior gap that prevents many raw ideas from maturing into richer concepts.

28 CROSSING THE CHASM

Too many ideas just don't make it. Not because they're bad, but because they didn't make it across the early idea chasm:

- *Ideas discarded too early*
- *Ideas not effectively captured*
- *Ideas not systematically evaluated*
- *Ideas evaluated in a too narrow context*
- *Ideas competing internally, but not always on fair terms*

As one "big idea" innovation is a relatively rare phenomenon, a stock of smaller but promising ideas is in most organizations a better base for commercializing creativity. By stimulating creativity, many ideas can be generated. This is good as creating many ideas increases the chance of creating some good ideas.

However, in the pursuit of new opportunities, too many ideas may be quickly dismissed as having too little value or being not practical, too costly or too risky.

In addition, and quite naturally, most organizations look at potential opportunities from the perspective of their current business. These well known behaviors may prevent many ideas from maturing into potentially valuable concepts.

To ensure that more ideas get a chance to mature, organizations need to level the playing field and be better equipped to identify ideas that can turn into good business — now or in the future. Working with *idea portfolios* serves this purpose.

29 IN THE PORTFOLIO

Can we put this idea in the portfolio?

In the afternoon. I've got my lunch sandwich in it now

© Anders Hemre

An idea portfolio can be defined as an organized and managed intangible asset of new product or service concepts with potential, but not yet realized, business value. The content of the portfolio represents intellectual capital and should be viewed not just as a collection of ideas with business potential, but also as an important record of creative and collaborative thinking and as a rich resource for business development.

A portfolio approach to idea management aligns such practices with those used for product and project portfolios. An idea taken from the portfolio would be well prepared to enter the front end of the development pipeline should a decision be made to go ahead with the development of a new product or service. Also, an idea that was originally rated at medium or low potential could be reconsidered later if events or circumstances so demand. In such a case, the idea portfolio would provide all the necessary background information assuming that the associated knowledge (idea) records have been kept and can be easily retrieved.

Ideas can be generated in both serendipitous and deliberate ways during activities such as team brainstorming sessions, individual creative thinking, peer discussions or organized idea campaigns. It is likely that the best return on creativity results from directing the effort towards certain business issues rather than just trying to stimulate idea generation in general.

Once generated, ideas should be allowed to incubate for some time before they are ready to be evaluated. Idea incubation may involve organized activities such as idea clustering, idea enhancement and idea collaboration.

As each single new idea may not carry enough merit on its own, the deliberate clustering of ideas provides the opportunity to create richer concepts by combining two or more ideas.

Further developing individual ideas or idea clusters through enhancement and collaboration activities will require the participation of not only the idea originators, but also peers, key managers and domain experts. In order to facilitate a richer dialogue, ideas may need to be enhanced through e.g. visualization or be described in user scenarios.

Organizations that have dedicated mechanisms for innovation, collaboration and knowledge sharing in place, such as e.g. *innovation cells, expert networks* or *communities of practice,* could use these to facilitate the process. It will involve not just a search for the next big idea but could create an environment of "micro innovation" where profitable growth may also come from the implementation of many small ideas.

> *"A well managed idea portfolio*
> *is an intellectual capital asset and*
> *should be accounted for."*

Despite the obvious benefits they bring to organizations, if not regularly used and updated, idea portfolios run the risk of becoming outdated and obsolete. It could be the task of an *idea portfolio manager* to ensure that the portfolio not only serves as an historical record, but actually keeps delivering value. And that it is accounted for.

30 STACKING UP

All ideas may not be suitable for implementation and ideas will of course also compete for development resources. Therefore, each idea needs to be subject to an evaluation using a set of predetermined criteria involving both opportunity value and implementation considerations. That way, ideas will not just be compared with one another, but rated against a set of criteria derived from strategy, business objectives and organizational capabilities.

Opportunity value would be estimated depending on business factors such as

- Strategic fit
- Customer value
- Business potential
- Competitive advantage
- Impact on current business

It is important to note that the purpose at this point is not to do full ROI calculations on ideas, but rather to rate all ideas against defined criteria to get a first assessment of business potentials and challenges. It is the result of these initial idea evaluations along with descriptions of the ideas themselves that make up the content of an idea portfolio.

Implementation considerations would typically include

- Cost & complexity
- Technology availability
- Intellectual property rights
- Resource & value chain impact
- Knowledge & skills requirements

In this evaluation process, the separation of opportunity value from implementation considerations such as e.g. cost & complexity is crucial to avoid the premature discounting of opportunity value due to the perceived challenges involved.

Even if the analysis at this point is not very deep or detailed, individuals with particular expertise need to be involved. Deep domain expertise is acquired through years of deliberate practice and is demonstrated by the effectiveness and fluency in complex problem solving and by the ability to see high value opportunities through a wider range of perspectives and a richer repertoire of insights.

Experts thus play an important role not just as creative thinkers and complex problem solvers, but also as management advisors.

Managers may have been involved during the early ideation stage, but their key role is to decide which opportunities should be pursued and organize the effort accordingly.

This will obviously benefit not only from good advice but also from applying a good methodology and making good value assessments of potential projects.

31 CHOOSING WISELY

After the initial evaluation, for each idea four basic options exist: *farm out, commit & commercialize, engage & learn* or *watch & wait,* where the last two represent options to delay a full investment. Each positioning alternative needs to include clearly identified exit options.

The choice is a management decision that can, in addition to relying on the initial idea review discussed above, be supported by a product or technology SWOT analysis, competitive intelligence (CI) and market research.

In this context, "watch and wait" is not the same thing as "wait and see". It's an *active monitoring* of the opportunity ensuring that the organization can decide and move quickly at a later point in time. "Engage and learn" would involve a limited investment in e.g. experimentation or a pilot project.

A decision to "commit and commercialize", i.e. launch a development project and go to market, can be made directly or after a delay by choosing one of the other options first. In either case, a decision to go ahead must be based on a good estimate of project value.

32 ACCOUNTING FOR IDEAS

The value of a specific innovation, i.e. the expected gains from going to market with an idea, is basically determined as the value of the opportunity involved less the cost of implementation. In financial terms this is often calculated using discounted cash flows (DCF) such as net present value (NPV).

Although straightforward to apply, it is well known that traditional NPV calculations may undervalue innovation by

- assuming that not investing results in unchanged business performance
- not accounting for management flexibility
- not accounting for potential growth options
- not valuing delay and uncertainty

Such considerations can be taken into account by using real options valuation.

An *option* is the right, but not the obligation, to buy or sell an asset in the future at a fixed (prenegotiated) price. Options are financial derivatives traded in (financial) markets.

A *real option* is the right, but not the obligation, to invest in a business opportunity or choose a particular course of action for developing, growing or abandoning an opportunity.

In R&D, the (real) option is to develop a new technology or product, the investment is the project and the (underlying) asset is the future cash flows from product sales.

Unlike financial options, real options are not traded in a market.

The Black-Scholes formula used in options pricing can be applied to the valuation of innovation, but is mathematically quite a bit more involved than the rather simple DCF calculations. In particular it uses a normally distributed probability function to capture the uncertainty (volatility) of estimates.

Understandably, most innovation managers will freeze when they see it.

In financial markets a lot of information is available concerning the volatility of assets. The variability (standard deviation) of future revenues from innovations can be difficult to determine. The Black-Scholes formula should therefore be applied with caution unless sufficient, relevant and reliable data from previous R&D projects is available for analysis.

Without using numerical calculations such as Black-Scholes, the concept of real options can still be applied in the valuation of innovation projects.

The following considerations could then be made using rough value estimates:

- *Uncertainty in revenue estimates (greater uncertainty has greater value)*
- *Possibility to stage development (e.g. VC funding in rounds)*
- *Possibility to scope up/down (modular development)*
- *Possibility to delay investment (the value of deferring a decision to develop)*
- *Technical flexibility (design architecture, buy/build options…)*
- *Reuse opportunities (platform, applications…)*
- *Future growth/expansion opportunities (options for additional investments)*
- *Exit opportunities (options to abandon a project)*

There are several trade-offs involved in valuating options.

The value of a delay must e.g. be weighed against missing a market window or losing a first mover advantage.

Technologies and markets eventually dictate when the investment in new development must be given priority over the reuse of existing components.

For a fair assessment of opportunity value, making the investment and creating real options should both be accounted for in the valuation of innovation and innovation project portfolios.

The total value of an innovation project is thus equal to

NPV + Investment Bonus + Options Premium

The investment bonus represents the value of avoiding a decline in business performance in case the investment is *not* made and the options premium is the value of having or creating real options.

The value estimates would be easier to do and turn out more accurate if the idea being pursued has been subject to an initial evaluation as part of creating the idea portfolio discussed above.

Applying real options thinking is particularly useful when traditional NPV is not strongly positive or when considerable uncertainty is present, e.g. when investing in emerging technologies.

In this way managing innovation portfolios can be seen as the exercising of a series of real options. By exercising or abandoning options, management can charter a course that maximizes the return — or minimizes the loss — on innovation.

One should remember that the valuation methods discussed are not meant to predict the future. They are only management tools used to decide whether to invest in a particular innovation or to choose between different innovation opportunities.

Obviously, NPV calculations and real options valuations do not address risk or uncertainty other than those associated with future revenues. In an actual R&D project, internal risks must of course still be assessed and managed in other ways.

33 FAILING TO MANAGE

The cases of Nokia and Kodak are well known. Whereas the demise of Kodak is already industry history, the case of Nokia is not over, but *something* certainly happened to the Finnish telecom company.

The same basic reasons may have dictated the fates of both companies. Despite the fact that both companies were full of smart people and people who understood what was happening, they were still unable to manage.

According to Chalmers University researcher Dr. Christian Sandström, these kinds of failures occur because:

- Big companies prioritize big markets
- Competence turns into incompetence
- Internal conflicts and issues take focus away from the external view
- Companies get stuck in the market's preferences
- Product architecture creates organizational lock-ins
- New ideas cannot find a landing strip
- Disruptive technology changes industry structures
- Traditional investment models discriminate against innovation

It's easy to agree. Maybe one could add the failure of some companies to recognize and exploit their own core competencies and understand their own value propositions.

Companies are usually organized according to existing markets and products, making it difficult for internal entrepreneurs to find room for new ideas and initiatives. Adding to the challenge, senior managers have most likely not been promoted for breaking rules and rocking boats or for failing fast with a new idea.

Further away from it, senior managers must learn to work with technologies and innovation through people.

Despite the obvious challenges involved, managers *can* organize and create conditions for innovation by creating expectation, making room and personally engage, not so much to manage in traditional ways but to serve the process by:

- Providing resources and support
- Communicating the importance
- Promoting risk tolerance

- Welcoming uncertainty
- Embracing change
- Asking questions
- Allowing time

The management challenge is doing what needs to be done for innovation, while dealing with the urgent demands and priorities of daily business as well.

The good news is that while innovation history is littered with failures, it also accounts for many great successes and many firms have demonstrated an unusually high capacity for innovation. Some could even be called super innovators.

34 SUPER INNOVATION

No doubt some firms are more innovative than others. They successfully exploit emerging technologies, create new markets and dominate their industries. It's not a coincidence that e.g. Apple repeatedly rates as a top innovator in surveys. Nor is it surprising to find that firms operating in innovative national or regional economies or in highly competitive industries have developed a stronger capacity to innovate than others or that a deliberate effort to manage the innovation process pays off in performance.

It may be less clear though what exactly the traits of highly innovative firms are. Innovation processes, practices and tools certainly play important roles in building capacity for innovation. Other factors such as access to funds, risk tolerance and management support also create conditions favorable to innovation, but highly innovative firms seem to have something more. They have adopted innovation as a business strategy.

Selecting an innovation strategy involves positioning innovation in the market and technology space and determining the level of effort required.

Most companies have adopted one or several of the following innovation approaches:

- Strategic innovator
- Intermittent innovator
- Technology modifier
- Technology adopter

Whatever innovation strategy chosen, it must eventually translate into reinforced competitiveness, superior value creation and increased business strength.

Apple's former CEO Steve Jobs once said, "I want to make a ding in the universe". Not a particularly humble wish, but almost typical of Apple's approach to doing business. They claim they don't do it by traditional market research, but by immersing themselves in user issues, wants and needs and ideas to the extent that they can say if we like it, others will too.
The people at Apple are not just obsessed with innovation, but are quite deliberate in the way they go about being innovative. The end result — as can be seen at the company's product launches — is almost as if they don't go to market with a new product, but the market comes to them.

When a motor vehicle firm recognizes its own core expertise as that of engineering and building not just motorbikes but combustion engines and power trains — as Honda did a long time ago — new opportunities emerge. Today, Honda is not only a large and successful motorcycle and car maker, but also a manufacturer of lawn mowers, tractors and other power equipment and a world leader in advanced robotics.

When Ericsson — a large telecommunications company — once stated that "it's about communication, the rest is technology" they were trying to look at themselves and their business from a broader perspective than simply being an equipment maker. For more than a decade, cellular phone makers have deliberately evolved their products from being wireless telephones to mobile lifestyle devices.

IBM became famous more than a decade ago for their online innovation jam reaching out across the entire organization and generating many thousands of ideas in a short period of time. Some were pursued and the company demonstrated that it's possible to create returns on creativity by being massively inclusive.
Open innovation may not be for everyone, but firms that succeed with external sourcing of ideas or with co-development of products can certainly gain a considerable advantage, like e.g. Proctor & Gamble with their connect & develop approach to innovation.

When Google encourages people to spend part of their time on ideas and projects of their choice, not only are they introducing and exploiting organizational slack, they are also sending a strong message that innovation matters. And they accelerate the development of future innovation leaders.

In general, a highly innovative firm could be described as one that sustains a strong market performance primarily through innovation. And studies confirm that innovative firms generally do better in their markets than non-innovative firms. However, even in an era of accelerated innovation and rapid creation of new markets, moderating forces will continue to be present — the resistance to change and natural risk aversion of individuals, organizations and societies as well as economic & financial conditions and the responsiveness of markets.

In summary, the highly innovative firm

- is good at what it does but wants to become even better
- has a real fear of complacency and status quo

- has a sense of urgency about being curious and creative
- is continuously directing the creative effort towards outcomes beneficial to the business
- has developed effective ways of combining creativity, expertise and management into a well orchestrated and highly productive innovation process
- is developing, encouraging and empowering individuals to act as innovation leaders
- has found effective ways of both exploring and accomplishing through dense and active networks
- is actively seeking new knowledge and is particularly good at exploiting incongruities, change and shifts in market forces
- is highly skilled in forming coalitions and alliances around a new idea
- is imagining the future and sees its mission as trying to make it happen

Both the average tenure of CEOs and the lifespan of enterprises have become shorter. Even if also highly innovative enterprises don't survive in the long run, chances are they may have left their mark on entire industries and created a great deal of value.

And they would have served as a strong inspiration to others — companies that also may go on to become truly creative.

35 THE CREATIVE COMPANY

Successful innovation requires understanding and promoting creativity, effective orchestration of the innovative effort and precision in finding a path to markets and profits.

> *"Creative companies don't just have more ideas.*
> *They also accomplish more with*
> *the ideas they have."*

Innovation based businesses need to stimulate and sustain the creative effort through a guided ideation process. They can benefit from using a portfolio approach to idea management in combination with a comprehensive project valuation method involving real options thinking. The outcome could be a project portfolio that most effectively closes the firm's estimated innovation gap and ensures that high value opportunities are not left unidentified or unaddressed.

Working in this way does not, however, eliminate innovation or project failures. In fact, failure is a necessary part of innovation as it identifies bad solutions and accelerates learning.

What the suggested approach *will* do is to help maximize the returns on creativity and on innovative effort, thereby accomplishing what all good innovation is aiming for - turning good ideas into good business. And that's what creative companies do.

COPYRIGHT – ABOUT THE AUTHOR

Anders Hemre is an independent business coach and management advisor with extensive international and cross-cultural experience having worked in various engineering and management capacities for the Ericsson group in Europe, the Middle East, the Far East and North America.
He currently lives in Gothenburg, Sweden, where he specializes in how organizations best work with strategy, innovation, knowledge and expertise. When time permits he cultivates his interests in art, history and science, enjoys reading Scandinavian crime novels and looks after his small but interesting collection of Chinese snuff bottles.

Anders is a MSEE graduate from the Chalmers University of Technology. He can be reached at

ahemre@kunskapsteknik.se

Visit him online at www.kunskapsteknik.se

A Brainovation® Book

This book is also available in e-book format (ISBN 978-1-988375-15-1), also with Amazon Kindle specific formatting (ISBN 978-1-988375-16-8) Coming later in 2018 as an audiobook (ISBN 978-1-988375-18-2)

Other books by Anders Hemre

THE COMPETENT COMPANY - Third Edition

"Competent companies are good at what they do. But it's when knowledge challenges generally held beliefs and when expertise challenges authority, that companies are put to the test – whether they can learn and change or whether they cannot."
Paperback (coming later in 2018) ISBN 978-1-988375-14-4

This book is also available in e-book format (ISBN 978-1-988375-12-0), also with Amazon Kindle specific formatting (ISBN 978-1-988375-13-7) Coming later in 2018 as an audiobook (ISBN 978-1-988375-19-9)

THE COMPETITIVE COMPANY - Third Edition

"Today, competition seems to be everywhere. At the same time, successful companies need to find effective ways to both collaborate and compete. In fact, a competitive company most likely is also one that collaborates well and is able to form productive partnerships."
Paperback (coming later in 2018) ISBN 978-1-988375-11-3

This book is also available in e-book format (ISBN 978-1-988375-09-0), also with Amazon Kindle specific formatting (ISBN 978-1-988375-10-6) Coming later in 2018 as an audiobook (ISBN 978-1-988375-20-5)

Paperback editing and publishing by Geoffrey B. Dahl & Associates Inc. (publish@geoffdahl.com) ©2018

THE CREATIVE COMPANY - Third Edition
ISBN 978-1-988375-17-5

www.ingramcontent.com/pod-product-compliance
Lightning Source LLC
Chambersburg PA
CBHW022049190326
41520CB00008B/754